Shell Scripting in Action

Real-world Examples and Case Studies

Owen Ford

Welcome to "Shell Scripting in Action: Real-world Examples and Case Studies"! I am thrilled to present this book to you, as it is the culmination of my passion for shell scripting and my desire to share practical knowledge and insights with fellow enthusiasts like yourself.

In today's fast-paced world, automation and efficiency are key factors in driving productivity and achieving success. And that's where shell scripting comes into play. Shell scripting provides a powerful toolset for automating tasks, managing systems, and processing data, making it an essential skill for system administrators, developers, and anyone seeking to leverage the full potential of the command-line interface.

This book takes a hands-on approach, focusing on real-world examples and case studies that demonstrate the practical application of shell scripting. Whether you are a beginner looking to master the fundamentals or an experienced user aiming to expand your scripting repertoire, this book is designed to provide you with the knowledge and skills necessary to tackle real-world challenges head-on.

Throughout the chapters, we will explore the core concepts of shell scripting, covering topics such as file and directory operations, text processing, system administration, network automation, data analysis, web development, and more. Each chapter will guide you through relevant examples and case studies, illustrating how shell scripting can be used to solve common problems and streamline daily workflows.

Moreover, we will delve into best practices for writing clean and maintainable scripts, error handling and debugging techniques, and advanced scripting concepts that will empower you to take your scripting skills to the next level. Additionally, we will explore the integration of shell scripting with other scripting languages and tools, as well as its potential for building robust applications and working within automation frameworks.

By the end of this book, you will not only have a solid understanding of shell scripting, but you will also have a repertoire of practical examples and case studies to draw from, empowering you to confidently apply your newfound knowledge to real-world scenarios.

So, whether you are a seasoned professional or a curious beginner, I invite you to embark on this exciting journey of exploring shell scripting in action. Together, let's unlock the full potential of the command-line interface and revolutionize the way we approach automation and efficiency.

Let's dive in and bring shell scripting to life!

Owen Ford

Chapter 1: Introduction to Shell Scripting................... 8
　　1.1 Understanding the basics of shell scripting........... 9
　　1.2 Differentiating between various shell environments (Bash, Zsh, etc.)..11
　　1.3 Setting up the shell environment: configuring prompts, aliases, and variables................................... 13

Chapter 2: Shell Scripting Basics................................ 16
　　2.1 Creating and running your first shell script........... 18
　　2.2 Working with variables: assigning values, variable substitution, and quoting... 20
　　2.3 Control flow: conditional statements (if-else, case), loops (for, while), and exit codes................................. 22

Chapter 3: File and Directory Operations.....................26
　　3.1 Navigating the file system: current directory, absolute and relative paths.. 28
　　3.2 Creating and managing files and directories: touch, mkdir, rm, mv, cp.. 30
　　3.3 File permissions and ownership: chmod, chown, chgrp.. 32

Chapter 4: Text Processing with Shell Scripts............ 35
　　4.1 Pattern matching: wildcards, globbing, and regular expressions... 37
　　4.2 Searching and replacing text in files: grep, sed, awk 39
　　4.3 Parsing structured files: using delimiter-based parsing and field extraction... 41

Chapter 5: Shell Scripting for System Administration 44
　　5.1 Automating system tasks: scheduling scripts with cron, managing user accounts................................... 46
　　5.2 Process and service management: starting, stopping, and monitoring processes.......................... 48
　　5.3 System resource monitoring: CPU, memory, disk usage, and log analysis... 51

Chapter 6: Working with Networks............................ 54
    6.1 Automating network-related tasks: pinging hosts, checking network connectivity..................................... 56
    6.2 Retrieving information from remote servers: SSH, SCP, and remote command execution........................ 58
    6.3 Network troubleshooting: tracing routes, analyzing network packets.. 61

Chapter 7: Shell Scripting for Data Analysis............... 64
    7.1 Processing and analyzing data files: sorting, filtering, and aggregation.. 66
    7.2 Working with CSV, JSON, and XML data: parsing and manipulating structured data............................... 68
    7.3 Generating reports and visualizations: text-based reports and simple charts.. 70

Chapter 8: Scripting for Web Development................. 73
    8.1 Web scraping and data extraction: using curl, wget, and regex... 75
    8.2 Automating website testing: simulating user interactions with tools like Selenium........................... 77
    8.3 Interacting with APIs: making HTTP requests and processing API responses... 79

Chapter 9: Shell Scripting Best Practices.................... 82
    9.1 Writing clean and maintainable scripts: code formatting and commenting.. 85
    9.2 Error handling and debugging: handling errors, logging, and troubleshooting....................................... 87
    9.3 Script optimization and performance considerations: improving execution speed and efficiency... 90

Chapter 10: Real-world Examples and Case Studies..94
    10.1 Case study 1: Automating backups and data synchronization with rsync.. 96
    10.2 Case study 2: Creating a log analysis script with grep and awk... 100
    10.3 Case study 3: Building a deployment pipeline with

shell scripting and Git... 103

Chapter 11: Advanced Shell Scripting Techniques... 108

11.1 Advanced features of Bash scripting: arrays, functions, and process substitution........................... 111

11.2 Script modularity and code reuse: creating libraries and modular scripts....................................... 113

11.3 Scripting for security and defensive programming: input validation and secure coding practices............ 116

Chapter 12: Beyond Shell Scripting............................120

12.1 Integration with other scripting languages and tools: using Python, Perl, or Ruby........................... 123

12.2 Creating shell script-based applications: packaging scripts as executables........................... 126

12.3 Exploring advanced automation frameworks: Ansible, Chef, and Puppet.. 129

Chapter 1: Introduction to Shell Scripting

Welcome to the exciting world of shell scripting! In this chapter, we will lay the foundation for your journey into the realm of automation, efficiency, and command-line mastery. Whether you are a beginner eager to learn the basics or an experienced user looking to expand your scripting skills, this chapter will serve as your gateway into the world of shell scripting.

We will begin by gaining a solid understanding of what shell scripting is and why it holds such importance in the realm of computing. You will discover how shell scripting empowers you to automate repetitive tasks, streamline workflows, and unlock the full potential of the command-line interface.

Next, we will explore different shell environments, such as Bash, Zsh, and others, enabling you to make an informed choice based on your needs and preferences. We will guide you through the process of setting up your shell environment, including configuring prompts, aliases, and variables, to enhance your scripting experience and increase productivity.

As we embark on this chapter, it is important to remember that while shell scripting can be a powerful tool, it is also accessible to beginners. We will provide a gentle introduction to the concepts and terminology used in shell scripting, ensuring that you can grasp the fundamentals and build a strong foundation for your scripting journey.

So, whether you are a system administrator, a developer, or simply someone seeking to elevate their command-line skills, get ready to immerse yourself in the world of shell scripting. Throughout this chapter and the ones to follow, we will equip you with the knowledge, skills, and practical examples to become proficient in creating efficient and effective shell scripts.

Get ready to unleash the power of the command line as we dive into Chapter 1: Introduction to Shell Scripting. Let's embark on this exciting adventure together and unlock the vast potential of automation and efficiency through shell scripting!

1.1 Understanding the basics of shell scripting

Understanding the basics of shell scripting is crucial for anyone interested in automating tasks and efficiently managing their system. Shell scripting involves writing scripts that leverage the command-line interface of an operating system to execute a series of commands. It provides a way to combine multiple commands, control their execution flow, and perform operations on files, directories, and data streams.

To grasp the basics, one must familiarize themselves with the shell environment, such as Bash, and its syntax. This includes understanding variables, command substitution, input/output redirection, and control structures like loops and conditionals. Additionally, learning about shell built-in commands and their parameters expands the scripting capabilities.

An essential aspect of shell scripting is understanding how to handle command-line arguments passed to a script, enabling user interaction and customization. Moreover, utilizing functions enables code modularity and reusability.

File manipulation is a fundamental aspect of shell scripting. Mastering commands like cat, grep, sed, and awk enables efficient text processing, pattern matching, and data extraction.

A crucial skill is handling error conditions and performing error checking to ensure robust and reliable scripts. This includes checking return codes, handling exceptions, and implementing logging mechanisms.

Lastly, understanding the concept of environment variables and using them to store configuration data or provide information to scripts greatly enhances their versatility.

By grasping the basics of shell scripting, individuals gain the ability to automate repetitive tasks, streamline workflows, and create powerful scripts that boost productivity and system management efficiency.

1.2 Differentiating between various shell environments (Bash, Zsh, etc.)

Differentiating between various shell environments, such as Bash, Zsh, and others, is important to understand the nuances and features offered by each shell. While they share commonalities as command-line interfaces, they have distinct characteristics that impact scripting and user experience.

Bash (Bourne Again SHell) is one of the most popular and widely used shells. It is the default shell on many Unix-like systems, including Linux. Bash provides extensive compatibility with the POSIX shell standard and offers a rich set of features, including command-line editing, history management, programmable completion, and advanced scripting capabilities.

Zsh (Z Shell) is another powerful shell with additional features and customization options. It includes advanced interactive features, such as enhanced tab completion, spelling correction, and globbing options. Zsh also supports powerful themes and plugins, making it highly customizable for user preferences.

Other shell environments, like Korn Shell (ksh), C Shell (csh), and Fish (Friendly Interactive SHell), have their own distinct features and syntax. Ksh provides a robust scripting language and features like associative arrays, command-line editing, and job control. Csh and its improved variant, Tcsh, offer interactive features, history expansion, and a C-like syntax. Fish focuses on user-friendliness and offers syntax highlighting, autosuggestions, and powerful tab completion.

Differentiating between these shell environments involves understanding their syntax differences, interactive features, scripting capabilities, and available options for customization. Users can choose a shell based on their personal preferences, the specific requirements of a task, or the compatibility with their system.

It's worth noting that while shell scripting principles generally apply across different environments, certain commands, syntax, or built-in features may vary. Therefore, it is essential to consider the specific shell environment when writing scripts or configuring user preferences.

By recognizing the distinctions between shell environments, individuals can leverage the strengths and features of each shell to enhance their command-line experience, optimize scripting practices, and tailor their workflow to suit their needs.

1.3 Setting up the shell environment: configuring prompts, aliases, and variables

Setting up the shell environment involves configuring prompts, aliases, and variables to personalize and enhance the user experience. These customizations make the shell more efficient, provide helpful information, and streamline command execution. Here's an overview of each aspect:

Prompts:

The prompt is the text displayed before the command input. Customizing the prompt allows users to display useful information like the current working directory, username, hostname, time, or any other desired details. Modifying the prompt can be done by setting the PS1 variable in the shell configuration file (.bashrc, .zshrc, etc.).

Aliases:

Aliases are shortcuts or abbreviations for commonly used commands or command sequences. They save time and typing effort. For example, creating an alias like "alias ll='ls -al'" would make "ll" equivalent to "ls -al". Aliases can be defined in the shell configuration file, and they are typically set using the alias command or by editing the shell configuration file directly.

Variables:

Shell variables store values that can be referenced and manipulated within scripts or the interactive shell session. They can be used to store configuration data, customize behavior, or provide input to scripts. Environment variables are accessible to all child processes spawned from the shell. Variables can be defined by using the variable name followed by an equal sign and the desired value, such as "VARNAME=value". Environment variables are often set in the shell configuration file.

To configure these aspects, follow these general steps:

- Identify the appropriate shell configuration file for your shell (e.g., .bashrc for Bash, .zshrc for Zsh).
- Open the configuration file using a text editor.
- Locate the section for customizations or add one if it doesn't exist.

- Set the desired values for the prompts, aliases, and variables using the appropriate syntax.

Save the configuration file and restart the shell or execute the file to apply the changes.

By customizing prompts, aliases, and variables, users can create a tailored shell environment that suits their preferences and workflow. These customizations enhance productivity, provide helpful information, and simplify command execution, ultimately making the shell more efficient and user-friendly.

Chapter 2: Shell Scripting Basics

In this chapter, we will dive deeper into the fundamentals of shell scripting. Building upon the foundation laid in Chapter 1, we will explore the essential elements and techniques that form the backbone of shell scripting. By understanding these basics, you will gain the confidence and knowledge needed to create powerful and efficient scripts.

We will start by guiding you through the process of creating and running your first shell script. You will learn the structure and syntax of a shell script, allowing you to write your own scripts from scratch. Through practical examples and step-by-step instructions, you will see how to harness the power of the command line to automate tasks and accomplish complex operations.

Variables are a crucial aspect of shell scripting, and we will dedicate a significant portion of this chapter to understanding their usage. You will learn how to assign values to variables, manipulate them through variable substitution, and ensure proper quoting to handle different types of data. Mastering variables is key to creating dynamic and adaptable scripts.

Control flow is another essential concept in shell scripting, enabling you to make decisions and repeat actions based on specific conditions. We will explore conditional statements, such as if-else and case, which allow your scripts to respond intelligently to different scenarios. Additionally, we will cover different loop structures, including for and while loops, empowering you to iterate over sets of data and automate repetitive tasks.

Throughout the chapter, we will emphasize best practices for writing clean and readable code. You will learn about code formatting conventions, proper commenting, and the importance of creating self-documenting scripts. These practices will not only enhance the readability of your scripts but also facilitate collaboration with other scripters and make maintenance a breeze.

By the end of this chapter, you will have a solid understanding of the fundamental building blocks of shell scripting. Armed with this knowledge, you will be prepared to tackle more complex scripting challenges and explore the vast capabilities of shell scripting in the subsequent chapters.

So, let's roll up our sleeves and delve into Chapter 2: Shell Scripting Basics. Together, we will master the core concepts that will serve as the bedrock of your shell scripting journey. Get ready to unlock the true potential of shell scripting and transform your command-line experience!

2.1 Creating and running your first shell script

Creating and running your first shell script is an exciting step towards automating tasks and leveraging the power of scripting. Follow these steps to create and execute your script:

Choose a text editor:

Select a text editor of your choice to write the shell script. Common options include Notepad++, Sublime Text, Visual Studio Code, or the terminal-based editors like Vim or Nano.

Open a new file:

Open a new file in your chosen text editor. Give it a meaningful name with the ".sh" extension, such as "myscript.sh". The ".sh" extension indicates that it is a shell script.
Set the shebang:

Start your script with a shebang line, which tells the system which shell should be used to interpret the script. For example, use "#!/bin/bash" for Bash scripts or "#!/bin/zsh" for Zsh scripts. Place this line at the top of your script file.

Write your script:

Begin writing your script's commands and logic below the shebang line. This can include any valid shell commands, such as assigning values to variables, executing commands, performing operations on files or directories, and more. Consider the specific task or functionality you want your script to accomplish.

Save the script:

Save the script file after writing the desired code. Make sure to save it with the ".sh" extension to indicate that it is a shell script.
Set execute permissions:

Before running the script, ensure it has execute permissions. In the terminal, navigate to the directory containing the script file and use the command "chmod +x myscript.sh" to grant executable permissions. Replace "myscript.sh" with the actual filename.

Execute the script:

To run your script, open a terminal, navigate to the directory containing the script, and enter "./myscript.sh" (replace "myscript.sh" with the actual filename). The "./" specifies that the script should be executed from the current directory. Alternatively, you can provide the full path to the script.
Verify the output:

After executing the script, observe the output in the terminal. It should display any messages or results produced by the commands within the script.

Congratulations! You have created and run your first shell script. Experiment with different commands, variables, and logic to explore the capabilities of shell scripting further. Shell scripts can save time, automate tasks, and enhance productivity by executing multiple commands in a structured and repeatable manner.

2.2 Working with variables: assigning values, variable substitution, and quoting

Working with variables is a fundamental aspect of shell scripting, enabling you to store and manipulate data. Here are the key concepts related to variables: assigning values, variable substitution, and quoting.

Assigning values to variables:

To assign a value to a variable, use the syntax: variable_name=value. For example, name="John" assigns the value "John" to the variable name. It's important not to include spaces around the equal sign.

Accessing variable values:

To access the value of a variable, prefix the variable name with a dollar sign ($). For example, echo $name will output the value stored in the name variable.

Variable substitution:

Variable substitution allows you to use the value of a variable within strings or commands. Use the syntax ${variable_name} or $variable_name for simple cases. For example, echo "My name is ${name}" or echo "My name is $name" will substitute the value of the name variable in the string.

Quoting variables:

Quoting is important when working with variables that contain spaces or special characters. There are three types of quotes:

- Double quotes (") preserve variable substitution and allow for the inclusion of spaces within a single variable. For example, echo "Hello, $name" will display "Hello, John".
- Single quotes (') preserve the literal value of all characters within the quotes. Variable substitution does not occur within single quotes. For example, echo 'Hello, $name' will display "Hello, $name" literally.

- Backticks (` `` `) allow command substitution, where the output of a command is substituted into the script. For example, current_date=`date +%Y-%m-%d` will assign the current date to the current_date variable.

Understanding variable assignment, substitution, and quoting is crucial for manipulating and utilizing data effectively within shell scripts. By mastering these concepts, you can perform dynamic operations, generate dynamic output, and handle variables with special characters or spaces accurately.

2.3 Control flow: conditional statements (if-else, case), loops (for, while), and exit codes

Control flow is a vital aspect of shell scripting, allowing you to make decisions, iterate over data, and handle the execution of your script. Here are the key elements of control flow in shell scripting: conditional statements, loops, and exit codes.

Conditional statements:

The if-else statement allows you to perform different actions based on a condition's evaluation. The syntax is as follows:

if [condition]; then
   # code to execute if the condition is true
else
   # code to execute if the condition is false
fi

You can use various operators within the condition, such as equality (==), inequality (!=), numerical comparisons (-lt, -gt, etc.), file tests (-e, -f, etc.), and more.

The case statement provides multiple condition checks using pattern matching. The syntax is as follows:

case "$variable" in
  pattern1)
    # code to execute if pattern1 matches
    ;;
  pattern2)
    # code to execute if pattern2 matches
    ;;
  *)
    # code to execute if no pattern matches
    ;;
esac

Patterns can include wildcards (*), character ranges ([a-z]), and more.

Loops:

The for loop allows you to iterate over a list of values or elements. The syntax is as follows:

for variable in value1 value2 value3; do
    # code to execute for each value
done

The while loop executes a block of code repeatedly as long as a condition is true. The syntax is as follows:

while [condition]; do
    # code to execute while the condition is true
done

Exit codes:

- Every command in a shell script returns an exit code to indicate its execution status. An exit code of 0 typically represents success, while non-zero codes indicate errors or specific conditions.
- You can check the exit code of the previous command using the special variable $?. For example, $? contains the exit code of the last executed command.

Understanding conditional statements, loops, and exit codes enables you to control the flow of your script based on conditions, iterate over data, and handle errors or specific outcomes. Utilize these control flow elements to build robust and dynamic scripts that can handle various scenarios and automate complex tasks.

Chapter 3: File and Directory Operations

In the world of shell scripting, manipulating files and directories is a fundamental skill. Whether you're managing data, organizing files, or automating system tasks, understanding file and directory operations is essential. In this chapter, we will explore a range of powerful commands and techniques that will enable you to navigate, create, modify, and manipulate files and directories with ease.

We will begin by familiarizing ourselves with the basics of navigating the file system. You will learn how to work with paths, differentiate between the current directory and absolute and relative paths, and navigate directories efficiently. Understanding these concepts will lay the groundwork for effective file and directory manipulation.

Creating and managing files and directories is a common task in shell scripting. We will cover essential commands such as touch, mkdir, rm, mv, and cp, providing you with the tools to create, remove, rename, move, and copy files and directories. Additionally, we will delve into techniques for handling file permissions and ownership, ensuring security and access control within your scripts.

As we progress, we will explore advanced file and directory operations, such as working with file globbing and wildcards. These powerful techniques allow you to target specific sets of files based on patterns and perform bulk operations on them. You will also learn how to use commands like find to search for files based on various criteria and perform actions on the matching results.

Efficiently managing file and directory operations requires understanding and manipulating file metadata. We will cover commands that provide information about files, such as ls, stat, and file, enabling you to extract details like file size, permissions, ownership, and file type. These commands are invaluable when developing scripts that require specific file characteristics or perform actions based on file properties.

Throughout the chapter, we will reinforce good scripting practices, emphasizing error handling and dealing with edge cases. You will learn how to gracefully handle situations where files or directories may not exist, and how to validate user input to ensure the smooth execution of your scripts.

By the end of this chapter, you will have a solid understanding of file and directory operations in shell scripting. Armed with this knowledge, you will be ready to tackle real-world challenges involving file manipulation, organization, and automation. So, let's dive into Chapter 3: File and Directory Operations and unlock the power of shell scripting to effectively manage your files and directories!

3.1 Navigating the file system: current directory, absolute and relative paths

Navigating the file system is essential when working with files and directories in shell scripting. Understanding the concepts of the current directory, absolute paths, and relative paths is crucial. Let's explore these concepts:

Current directory:

- The current directory refers to the directory in which you are currently located or working. When you open a terminal or execute a script, your current directory is initially set to your home directory.
- You can determine the current directory by using the pwd command, which stands for "print working directory."

Absolute paths:

- An absolute path provides the complete location of a file or directory starting from the

root directory. It specifies the full directory path from the root directory to the desired file or directory.
- Absolute paths always begin with a forward slash (/). For example, /home/user/documents/file.txt is an absolute path indicating the location of the file.txt file within the documents directory in the user's home directory.

Relative paths:

- Relative paths specify the location of a file or directory relative to the current directory. Instead of starting from the root directory, they start from the current directory.
- Relative paths can be expressed in two ways:
- The first is using a file or directory's name directly when it is located in the current directory. For example, if you are in the /home/user directory, file.txt refers to the file.txt file in the current directory.
- The second is using special notations to navigate up or down the directory tree. These notations include:
- . (dot) represents the current directory.
- .. (double dot) represents the parent directory.
- ../somedir refers to the directory "somedir" in the parent directory.
- ../../somedir refers to the directory "somedir" two levels up in the directory tree.

Understanding the current directory, absolute paths, and relative paths allows you to effectively navigate and reference files and directories within your shell scripts. By using the appropriate path conventions, you can access and manipulate the desired files and directories accurately and efficiently.

3.2 Creating and managing files and directories: touch, mkdir, rm, mv, cp

Creating and managing files and directories are common operations in shell scripting. Here are the key commands for creating, deleting, moving, and copying files and directories:

Creating files:

The touch command creates an empty file or updates the access and modification timestamps of an existing file. Usage: touch filename. For example, touch file.txt creates a new file named "file.txt" in the current directory.

Creating directories:

The mkdir command creates a new directory. Usage: mkdir directoryname. For example, mkdir mydir creates a new directory named "mydir" in the current directory.

Removing files and directories:

- The rm command is used to remove files and directories. Usage:
- To remove a file: rm filename. For example, rm file.txt removes the file named "file.txt".
- To remove a directory and its contents recursively: rm -r directoryname. For example, rm -r mydir removes the directory named "mydir" and all its contents.

Moving files and directories:

- The mv command is used to move files and directories. Usage:
- To move a file to a new location or rename a file: mv source destination. For example, mv file.txt newdir/ moves the file "file.txt" to the "newdir" directory.
- To move a directory to a new location or rename a directory: mv sourcedir destination. For example, mv mydir newlocation/ moves the directory "mydir" to the "newlocation" directory.

Copying files and directories:

- The cp command is used to copy files and directories. Usage:

- To copy a file to a new location: cp source destination. For example, cp file.txt newdir/ creates a copy of "file.txt" in the "newdir" directory.
- To copy a directory and its contents recursively: cp -r sourcedir destination. For example, cp -r mydir newlocation/ creates a copy of the "mydir" directory and all its contents in the "newlocation" directory.

These commands provide the necessary tools to create, delete, move, and copy files and directories in your shell scripts. Understanding and utilizing these commands effectively will enable you to manage file and directory operations efficiently.

3.3 File permissions and ownership: chmod, chown, chgrp

File permissions and ownership play a crucial role in ensuring the security and accessibility of files and directories in a shell scripting environment. Here are the key commands for managing file permissions and ownership:

Changing file permissions:

The chmod command is used to change the permissions of a file or directory. Permissions are represented by three sets of three characters: user permissions, group permissions, and other permissions.

Numeric notation: You can use numeric values to set permissions. Each permission is represented by a number:

- Read (4)
- Write (2)
- Execute (1)

For example, chmod 755 filename grants the owner read, write, and execute permissions (7), and read and execute permissions to the group and others (5).

Changing file ownership:

The chown command changes the owner of a file or directory. Usage: chown newowner filename. For example, chown user1 file.txt changes the owner of "file.txt" to "user1".

Changing group ownership:

The chgrp command changes the group ownership of a file or directory. Usage: chgrp newgroup filename. For example, chgrp group1 file.txt changes the group ownership of "file.txt" to "group1".

These commands allow you to manage file permissions and ownership, ensuring that files and directories are accessible and secure. Understanding and appropriately setting permissions and ownership is essential for maintaining the integrity and confidentiality of your data in a shell scripting environment.

Chapter 4: Text Processing with Shell Scripts

In the world of shell scripting, the ability to process and manipulate text is a crucial skill. Whether you're analyzing log files, parsing structured data, or searching for specific patterns, mastering text processing techniques will empower you to extract valuable insights and automate tasks efficiently. In this chapter, we will explore various tools and commands that will enable you to harness the power of shell scripting for text manipulation.

We will start by diving into the realm of pattern matching. You will learn about wildcards, also known as globbing, which allow you to match files and text based on patterns and perform operations on them. Additionally, we will explore regular expressions, a powerful tool for advanced pattern matching and text manipulation. You will discover how to use regular expressions to search for specific patterns, extract information, and perform substitutions.

Searching and replacing text in files is a common task in text processing. We will cover the versatile grep command, which enables you to search for specific patterns within files and filter text based on criteria. You will also learn about the powerful sed command, which not only allows you to search and replace text but also provides advanced text transformation capabilities. Additionally, we will explore the awk command, which excels at processing structured text and extracting specific fields based on delimiters.

Parsing structured files is another critical aspect of text processing. You will learn techniques for handling delimiter-based parsing, where you can split text into fields based on specific separators. We will explore the various ways you can extract and manipulate data within structured files, such as CSV, JSON, and XML. These skills will prove invaluable when working with data-intensive scripts and automating data processing tasks.

Throughout the chapter, we will emphasize the importance of script efficiency and performance. You will learn techniques for optimizing text processing operations, such as leveraging command options, using pipelines effectively, and minimizing unnecessary processing steps. These optimizations will ensure that your scripts run efficiently, even when dealing with large amounts of text data.

By the end of this chapter, you will have a strong grasp of text processing techniques in shell scripting. You will be equipped with the tools and knowledge necessary to search, filter, transform, and extract information from text files efficiently. So, let's embark on this text-processing journey together and explore the power of shell scripts in Chapter 4: Text

Processing with Shell Scripts. Get ready to unleash the potential of your text data!

4.1 Pattern matching: wildcards, globbing, and regular expressions

Pattern matching is a powerful feature in shell scripting that allows you to perform operations on multiple files or directories based on specific patterns. There are three common methods of pattern matching: wildcards, globbing, and regular expressions. Let's explore each of these:

Wildcards:

- Wildcards are characters that represent one or more other characters. They are used to match filenames or strings based on a specific pattern.
- The most commonly used wildcards are:
- * (asterisk): Matches any number of characters (including none).
- ? (question mark): Matches a single character.
- [ ] (square brackets): Matches a single character from a specified range or set of characters. For example, [aeiou] matches any vowel.

- For example, if you have files named "file1.txt", "file2.txt", and "file3.txt", using the wildcard file*.txt will match all three files.

Globbing:

- Globbing is an extension of wildcard matching that allows you to match files or directories based on more complex patterns.
- Common globbing patterns include:
- *: Matches zero or more characters.
- ?: Matches a single character.
- [ ]: Matches a single character from a specified range or set of characters.
- { }: Matches any of the comma-separated patterns within the braces. For example, {*.txt, *.doc} matches files with either a .txt or .doc extension.
- !(pattern): Matches anything except the specified pattern.
- Globbing patterns are often used with commands like ls, cp, rm, or in shell scripts to perform operations on multiple files at once.

Regular expressions:

- Regular expressions (regex) provide a more advanced pattern matching capability. They are a sequence of characters that define a search pattern.

- Regular expressions allow for complex matching based on rules and metacharacters. Some common metacharacters include . (matches any character), ^ (matches the start of a line), $ (matches the end of a line), and many more.
- Regular expressions are used with commands like grep, sed, and awk to search, manipulate, or extract data based on specific patterns.

Understanding and utilizing pattern matching techniques like wildcards, globbing, and regular expressions can significantly enhance your ability to perform batch operations, search for specific files or data, and manipulate text patterns within shell scripts. Mastering these pattern matching methods will make your scripts more versatile and efficient.

4.2 Searching and replacing text in files: grep, sed, awk

Searching and replacing text in files is a common task in shell scripting. There are several powerful commands available for this purpose, including grep, sed, and awk. Let's explore each of these commands:

grep:

- The grep command is used to search for specific text patterns within files. It can be used to find lines that match a given pattern or to extract specific data from files.
- Usage: grep pattern file.
- Additional options can be used to modify the search behavior, such as ignoring case (-i), displaying line numbers (-n), searching recursively in directories (-r), and more.

sed:

- The sed command is a stream editor used for performing text transformations. It can be used to search for text patterns and replace them with new content.
- Usage: sed 's/pattern/replacement/' file.
- Additional options and commands can be used to modify the replacement behavior, such as performing global replacements (g flag), using regular expressions, specifying ranges of lines to operate on, and more.

awk:

- The awk command is a versatile programming language for manipulating text files. It can search for patterns, perform actions on matching lines, and extract specific fields from files.
- Usage: awk '/pattern/ { action }' file.

- awk allows you to define actions based on patterns, such as printing lines that match a pattern, modifying specific fields, performing calculations, and more.
- awk has a wide range of built-in functions and variables that provide powerful text processing capabilities.

These commands offer different approaches to searching and replacing text in files. Depending on your specific requirements, you can choose the most suitable command for your shell scripting needs. By mastering grep, sed, and awk, you can efficiently search for specific patterns, extract relevant data, and perform text transformations in your scripts.

4.3 Parsing structured files: using delimiter-based parsing and field extraction

When working with structured files, such as CSV (comma-separated values) or TSV (tab-separated values), parsing the data becomes essential. Shell scripting provides tools for delimiter-based parsing and field extraction to process structured files efficiently. Let's explore these techniques:

Delimiter-based parsing:

- Delimiter-based parsing involves using a specific character or sequence of characters as a delimiter to split the data into fields.
- The cut command is commonly used for delimiter-based parsing. It allows you to extract specific columns or fields from a file based on a delimiter.
- Usage: cut -d delimiter -f fields file.
- Example: cut -d ',' -f 2,4 file.csv extracts the second and fourth columns from a CSV file, assuming the delimiter is a comma.
- You can also use the awk command for delimiter-based parsing. It provides more flexibility and advanced field manipulation capabilities.
- Usage: awk -F delimiter '{ actions }' file.
- Example: awk -F ',' '{ print $2, $4 }' file.csv prints the second and fourth fields from a CSV file using a comma as the delimiter.

Field extraction:

- Field extraction involves extracting specific fields based on their position or pattern within the structured file.
- The awk command is commonly used for field extraction. It allows you to define patterns and actions to extract specific fields.
- Usage: awk '{ actions }' file.

- Example: awk '{ print $1, $3 }' file.txt prints the first and third fields from a file, assuming fields are separated by whitespace.
- If the structured file has a specific pattern or format, you can also use regular expressions with tools like grep or sed to extract relevant fields.
- Usage: grep pattern file | sed 's/pattern/replacement/'.

By using delimiter-based parsing and field extraction techniques, you can process structured files effectively in shell scripting. Whether you need to extract specific columns or fields, filter data based on patterns, or perform calculations on selected data, these techniques provide the necessary tools to manipulate structured file data efficiently.

Chapter 5: Shell Scripting for System Administration

System administration tasks often involve repetitive actions, configuration management, and monitoring various aspects of a system. Shell scripting provides a powerful toolkit for automating these tasks, enabling system administrators to streamline their workflows and maintain efficient and reliable systems. In this chapter, we will delve into the world of shell scripting for system administration, equipping you with the skills to automate common administrative tasks and manage your systems effectively.

We will begin by exploring system information retrieval and monitoring. You will learn how to gather essential details about your system, such as CPU usage, memory utilization, disk space, and network statistics. We will cover commands such as df, top, ps, and netstat, and demonstrate how to extract and process the information they provide. With this knowledge, you will be able to create scripts that proactively monitor system health and alert you to potential issues.

Automation is a key aspect of system administration, and shell scripting allows you to automate repetitive tasks with ease. We will discuss techniques for managing system configurations, including modifying system files, installing and updating packages, and creating user accounts. You will learn how to automate these processes using shell scripts, saving time and ensuring consistency across multiple systems.

System troubleshooting and error handling are critical skills for a system administrator. We will explore techniques for analyzing system logs, parsing error messages, and creating scripts that assist in troubleshooting common issues. By automating error detection and resolution steps, you will be able to respond quickly to system alerts and minimize downtime.

Effective system administration involves managing scheduled tasks and performing regular maintenance. We will cover tools such as cron and at, enabling you to automate task scheduling and execute scripts at specific times or intervals. You will also learn how to create scripts that perform system backups, log rotation, and other routine maintenance tasks.

Security is of utmost importance in system administration. We will discuss techniques for user management, password management, and file permission settings. You will learn how to create scripts that enforce security measures, such as password policies, user access controls, and file integrity checks.

Throughout the chapter, we will emphasize best practices for writing secure and efficient scripts. You will learn about code organization, error handling, logging, and script testing, ensuring that your scripts are robust and reliable in a production environment.

By the end of this chapter, you will have a solid foundation in shell scripting for system administration. Armed with this knowledge, you will be able to automate routine tasks, monitor system health, troubleshoot issues, and enhance the security of your systems. So, let's dive into Chapter 5: Shell Scripting for System Administration and unlock the power of automation and efficiency in managing your systems. Get ready to take control of your administrative tasks!

5.1 Automating system tasks: scheduling scripts with cron, managing user accounts

Automating system tasks is a fundamental aspect of shell scripting. It allows you to schedule scripts to run at specific times and automate repetitive tasks. Additionally, managing user accounts is crucial for system administration. Let's explore these topics in more detail:

Scheduling scripts with cron:

The cron utility is a time-based job scheduler in Unix-like operating systems. It enables you to schedule the execution of scripts or commands at predefined intervals.
To schedule a script with cron, you need to edit the cron table using the crontab command.

Usage: crontab -e (to edit the cron table).

The cron table uses a specific syntax to specify the timing and command for each scheduled task. For example, the following line schedules a script to run every day at 8:00 AM:

*0 8 * * * /path/to/script.sh*

You can schedule tasks at various intervals, such as hourly, daily, weekly, or even specific dates and times.

By utilizing cron, you can automate routine tasks, generate regular reports, perform backups, and more.

Managing user accounts:

Shell scripting enables you to automate user account management tasks, such as creating, modifying, or deleting user accounts.

The useradd command is used to create new user accounts, while usermod is used to modify existing accounts.

Usage:

Creating a new user: useradd username.

Modifying user account properties: usermod options username.

Deleting a user account: userdel username.

User account management tasks can include setting passwords, assigning home directories, managing user groups, and granting specific privileges.

Additionally, you can use the passwd command to change the password for a user account.

Automating system tasks with cron and managing user accounts through shell scripting significantly simplifies administrative tasks, enhances system efficiency, and ensures consistent management practices. By leveraging these capabilities, you can save time, streamline processes, and effectively manage system resources.

5.2 Process and service management: starting, stopping, and monitoring processes

Process and service management is an essential aspect of system administration, and shell scripting provides the tools to start, stop, and monitor processes effectively. Let's explore these concepts in more detail:

Starting processes:

- The start command is used to initiate a new process or service.
- Usage: start <command>.
- Example: start myscript.sh starts the execution of the script myscript.sh as a separate process.
- You can also use specific commands to start system services, such as service or systemctl, depending on your operating system.

Stopping processes:

- The stop command is used to terminate running processes.
- Usage: stop <process_id> or stop <process_name>.
- Example: stop 1234 terminates the process with the ID 1234.
- You can also use commands like kill or pkill to stop processes based on various criteria, such as process ID, process name, or process group.

Monitoring processes:

- The ps command allows you to monitor running processes and gather information about them.
- Usage: ps options.
- Common options include:
- aux: Display all processes running on the system.
- ef: Display processes in a hierarchical tree format.
- u: Display detailed information for each process.

Additionally, tools like top, htop, or pgrep provide more advanced process monitoring capabilities, including real-time updates, resource usage statistics, and process filtering.

Automating process and service management tasks through shell scripting allows you to streamline system administration, ensure proper startup and shutdown procedures, and effectively monitor the running processes. By leveraging these tools, you can automate routine tasks, improve system performance, and maintain the stability and availability of your system.

5.3 System resource monitoring: CPU, memory, disk usage, and log analysis

System resource monitoring is crucial for maintaining the health and performance of your system. Shell scripting provides various tools to monitor CPU usage, memory usage, disk usage, and analyze system logs. Let's explore these topics in more detail:

CPU monitoring:

- The top command provides real-time information about CPU usage, including a list of processes consuming the most CPU resources.
- Usage: top.
- Additional options can be used to sort processes based on CPU usage, update frequency, and more.
- You can redirect the output of top to a file for further analysis or use it within a shell script to automate monitoring tasks.

Memory monitoring:

- The free command displays information about memory usage, including total, used, and available memory.
- Usage: free.

- You can also use tools like top or htop to view memory usage of individual processes.
- Monitoring memory usage is important to identify potential memory leaks or excessive memory consumption.

Disk usage monitoring:

- The df command shows disk usage information for file systems mounted on your system.
- Usage: df.
- Additional options can be used to display usage in human-readable format, sort output, and specify file system types.
- Monitoring disk usage helps identify filesystems that are running out of space and may require cleanup or expansion.

Log analysis:

- System logs contain valuable information for monitoring and troubleshooting purposes.
- The grep command is commonly used to search for specific patterns or errors in log files.
- Usage: grep pattern logfile.
- You can automate log analysis by creating shell scripts that parse log files, extract relevant information, and generate reports or alerts based on specific conditions.

By incorporating system resource monitoring and log analysis into your shell scripts, you can automate the monitoring process, identify performance bottlenecks, detect anomalies, and take proactive measures to maintain system stability and optimize resource utilization.

Chapter 6: Working with Networks

In today's interconnected world, networking plays a vital role in the efficient functioning of systems and the exchange of information. As a shell scripter, having the ability to automate network-related tasks and troubleshoot network issues can significantly enhance your productivity. In this chapter, we will explore the power of shell scripting in the realm of networking, equipping you with the knowledge and tools to interact with networks effectively.

We will begin by understanding the basics of network communication. You will learn about IP addresses, subnetting, and network protocols, providing you with a solid foundation for network-related scripting. We will explore commands such as ifconfig, ip, and ping, enabling you to gather network information, configure network interfaces, and test network connectivity.

Automating network tasks is a key aspect of network administration. We will cover techniques for automating tasks such as network configuration, DNS management, and firewall rules. You will learn how to create scripts that interact with configuration files, modify network settings, and automate network-related changes across multiple systems.

Shell scripting also provides powerful capabilities for network monitoring and troubleshooting. We will explore commands such as netstat, tcpdump, and nmap, enabling you to analyze network traffic, monitor ports and services, and detect network anomalies. With these tools, you will be able to create scripts that proactively monitor network health, identify bottlenecks, and troubleshoot network issues.

Interacting with remote systems and servers is a common requirement in networking. We will explore techniques for remote access and automation, including SSH-based commands, remote file transfers, and executing commands on remote systems. You will learn how to create scripts that retrieve information from remote servers, perform automated backups, and execute commands across a network of systems.

Networking often involves working with APIs (Application Programming Interfaces) to interact with web services and retrieve information. We will cover techniques for making HTTP requests, parsing JSON responses, and extracting relevant data using tools like curl and jq. With these skills, you will be able to create scripts that interact with APIs, automate data retrieval, and integrate network operations with web-based services.

Throughout the chapter, we will emphasize best practices for network scripting, such as error handling, logging, and secure communication. You will also learn about techniques for scripting network security measures, including SSL/TLS encryption, secure file transfers, and authentication mechanisms.

By the end of this chapter, you will have the knowledge and skills to leverage shell scripting for network-related tasks, automation, and troubleshooting. You will be able to streamline network administration, proactively monitor network health, and interact with remote systems and web services. So, let's dive into Chapter 6: Working with Networks and unlock the power of shell scripting in the realm of networking. Get ready to conquer the world of network automation and efficiency!

6.1 Automating network-related tasks: pinging hosts, checking network connectivity

Automating network-related tasks is a valuable aspect of shell scripting, allowing you to perform tasks such as pinging hosts and checking network connectivity. Let's explore these concepts in more detail:

Pinging hosts:

- The ping command is commonly used to test network connectivity by sending ICMP echo requests to a specific host.
- Usage: ping host.
- You can specify options like the number of packets to send, the interval between packets, and the timeout period.
- By incorporating the ping command into a shell script, you can automate the process of pinging multiple hosts, recording the results, and generating reports.

Checking network connectivity:

- The nc (netcat) command is a versatile tool for checking network connectivity to a specific port on a host.
- Usage: nc -zv host port.
- This command attempts to establish a connection to the specified host and port. If successful, it indicates that the network connectivity is working.
- By scripting the nc command, you can check the connectivity to multiple hosts and ports, log the results, and perform further actions based on the connectivity status.

Network interface monitoring:

- The ifconfig or ip commands provide information about network interfaces and their configuration.
- Usage: ifconfig or ip <option>.
- You can extract details such as IP addresses, netmask, gateway, and other network interface parameters using these commands.
- By incorporating these commands into shell scripts, you can automate the monitoring of network interfaces, track changes, and generate notifications if necessary.

Automating network-related tasks through shell scripting helps you streamline network monitoring, diagnose connectivity issues, and perform routine checks. By leveraging tools like ping, nc, and network interface commands, you can save time, ensure network reliability, and effectively manage network-related tasks.

6.2 Retrieving information from remote servers: SSH, SCP, and remote command execution

Retrieving information from remote servers is a common task in shell scripting, and several tools are available to facilitate this process, including SSH, SCP, and remote command execution. Let's explore these concepts in more detail:

SSH (Secure Shell):

- SSH is a secure protocol used for establishing encrypted connections to remote servers.
- The ssh command allows you to log in to a remote server and execute commands remotely.
- Usage: ssh username@host.
- You can provide additional options to specify the port, use key-based authentication, or execute specific commands on the remote server.
- By incorporating ssh into your shell script, you can automate remote login, execute commands on remote servers, and retrieve output or data from those servers.

SCP (Secure Copy):

- SCP is a secure file transfer protocol that enables you to copy files between local and remote systems.
- The scp command allows you to transfer files securely between hosts.
- Usage: scp source_file destination.
- You can specify the remote host and location in the destination to copy files to a remote server.
- By utilizing scp within a shell script, you can automate file transfers between local and

remote systems, backup files to remote servers, or retrieve data from remote servers.

Remote command execution:

- In addition to SSH, tools like sshpass or expect can be used for automated remote command execution.
- sshpass allows you to provide the password as a parameter, enabling non-interactive authentication for automated scripts.
- Usage: sshpass -p password ssh username@host command.
- Similarly, expect allows you to automate interactions with remote systems, including entering passwords or responding to prompts.
- Usage: expect -c 'spawn ssh username@host command; expect "password:"; send "password\r"; interact'.
- These tools can be useful when automation requires handling authentication or interacting with prompts on remote servers.

By incorporating SSH, SCP, and remote command execution into your shell scripts, you can automate remote server management, retrieve information, transfer files securely, and execute commands on remote systems. These tools enhance efficiency, simplify remote operations, and facilitate the retrieval of data from remote servers.

6.3 Network troubleshooting: tracing routes, analyzing network packets

Network troubleshooting is a crucial task in maintaining network connectivity and resolving issues. Shell scripting provides tools to trace routes and analyze network packets, aiding in diagnosing and troubleshooting network problems. Let's explore these concepts in more detail:

Tracing routes:

- The traceroute command allows you to trace the route packets take from your computer to a destination host.
- Usage: traceroute destination_host.
- It displays the intermediate routers or hops along the path, helping you identify any network connectivity issues or delays.
- By incorporating traceroute into your shell script, you can automate the process of tracing routes to multiple hosts, record the results, and analyze the network paths.

Analyzing network packets:

- Wireshark is a powerful network packet analyzer that captures and analyzes network traffic in real-time.

- You can use the tshark command-line tool, a part of Wireshark, to capture and analyze network packets programmatically.
- Usage: tshark <options>.
- tshark provides various options to filter, dissect, and extract information from captured network packets.
- By scripting tshark within your shell script, you can automate packet capture, analyze network traffic, detect anomalies, and troubleshoot network issues.

Network interface statistics:

- The ifconfig or ip commands, mentioned earlier, also provide network interface statistics that can aid in troubleshooting network connectivity.
- Usage: ifconfig or ip <option>.
- You can extract information such as interface errors, dropped packets, and transmitted/received packet counts.
- Monitoring these statistics within your shell script can help identify network issues, monitor interface performance, and troubleshoot connectivity problems.

By incorporating route tracing, network packet analysis, and network interface statistics into your shell scripts, you can automate network troubleshooting tasks, identify potential issues, and diagnose network connectivity problems. These tools enhance your ability to monitor and troubleshoot network environments efficiently, improving network performance and reliability.

Chapter 7: Shell Scripting for Data Analysis

Data analysis is a critical skill in today's data-driven world, and shell scripting provides a versatile and efficient platform for performing various data analysis tasks. In this chapter, we will explore the realm of shell scripting for data analysis, equipping you with the tools and techniques to extract insights from data, automate analysis workflows, and make informed decisions.

We will start by understanding the basics of data manipulation using shell scripting. You will learn techniques for reading and writing data to files, handling different file formats such as CSV and JSON, and extracting specific data using commands like cut, grep, and awk. By mastering these foundational skills, you will be able to perform basic data extraction and transformation tasks.

One of the key aspects of data analysis is aggregating and summarizing data. We will cover techniques for grouping data, calculating statistics, and generating reports using commands such as sort, uniq, and wc. You will learn how to create scripts that automate data summarization and enable you to gain a high-level understanding of your data.

Shell scripting also provides powerful tools for filtering and querying data. We will explore commands like grep, awk, and sed that allow you to search for specific patterns, filter data based on criteria, and perform complex transformations. You will learn how to create scripts that efficiently extract relevant information from large datasets.

Performing calculations and numerical analysis is an important aspect of data analysis. We will cover techniques for performing mathematical operations, generating random numbers, and performing statistical analysis using commands like expr, bc, and datamash. You will be able to create scripts that automate calculations and derive meaningful insights from your data.

Visualization is a powerful tool for understanding and communicating data. We will explore techniques for creating simple plots and charts using commands like gnuplot and plotutils. You will learn how to generate visual representations of your data directly from your shell scripts, enabling you to gain insights at a glance.

Throughout the chapter, we will emphasize performance optimization and scalability when dealing with large datasets. You will learn techniques for efficiently processing and analyzing data, including leveraging parallel processing, optimizing loops, and using efficient data structures. These skills will enable you to handle large-scale data analysis tasks effectively.

By the end of this chapter, you will have a strong foundation in shell scripting for data analysis. You will be able to automate data extraction, transformation, summarization, and visualization tasks using shell scripts. So, let's dive into Chapter 7: Shell Scripting for Data Analysis and unlock the power of data-driven insights through efficient and scalable shell scripting. Get ready to unleash the potential of your data!

7.1 Processing and analyzing data files: sorting, filtering, and aggregation

Processing and analyzing data files is a common task in various domains, and shell scripting provides powerful tools for sorting, filtering, and aggregating data. Let's explore these concepts in more detail:

Sorting data:

- The sort command is used to sort data in a file based on specific criteria.
- Usage: sort <options> file.
- You can sort data alphabetically, numerically, in reverse order, or based on specific fields using delimiter options.

- By incorporating sort into your shell script, you can automate data sorting tasks, sort multiple files, and redirect sorted output to other files or processes.

Filtering data:

- The grep command allows you to filter data based on specific patterns or regular expressions.
- Usage: grep <options> pattern file.
- You can search for patterns, extract matching lines, or exclude lines that match specific patterns.
- Additionally, the awk command provides more advanced data filtering capabilities, allowing you to define complex conditions and perform actions on matching data.
- By combining grep and awk within your shell script, you can automate data filtering tasks, extract specific information from files, and generate reports based on filtered data.

Aggregating data:

- The awk command, along with other tools like cut, sed, and paste, can be used to aggregate and summarize data.
- You can use awk to calculate sums, averages, maximum or minimum values, or perform other

mathematical operations on specific columns or fields.
- Usage: awk <options> '{action}' file.
- By scripting these commands, you can automate data aggregation tasks, generate statistics, and create summary reports from large datasets.

By leveraging the sorting, filtering, and aggregating capabilities of tools like sort, grep, and awk, you can process and analyze data files effectively. Shell scripting allows you to automate these tasks, making it easier to work with large datasets, extract relevant information, and generate meaningful insights from your data.

7.2 Working with CSV, JSON, and XML data: parsing and manipulating structured data

Working with structured data formats like CSV, JSON, and XML is common in data processing tasks, and shell scripting provides tools to parse and manipulate such data efficiently. Let's explore these concepts in more detail:

CSV (Comma-Separated Values):

- The awk command is commonly used to parse and manipulate CSV data in shell scripts.
- You can specify the delimiter using the -F option to handle different delimiter formats (e.g., comma, tab).
- Usage: awk -F, '{actions}' file.csv.
- By using field variables like $1, $2, etc., you can access specific columns in the CSV file and perform operations or calculations.

JSON (JavaScript Object Notation):

- The jq command-line tool is a powerful tool for parsing and manipulating JSON data in shell scripts.
- Usage: jq '{filter}' file.json.
- jq provides a wide range of capabilities, including filtering, selecting specific fields, aggregating data, and transforming JSON structures.
- You can use jq to extract values, manipulate nested data, filter data based on conditions, and generate new JSON structures.

XML (eXtensible Markup Language):

- Tools like xmlstarlet and xmllint are commonly used for parsing and manipulating XML data in shell scripts.

- xmlstarlet provides a range of XML processing features, including querying, editing, and transforming XML files.
- Usage: xmlstarlet <options> <command> file.xml.
- You can use xmlstarlet to extract data from XML elements, modify values, perform XPath queries, and generate XML output.

By utilizing tools like awk, jq, xmlstarlet, and others, you can parse and manipulate structured data in formats like CSV, JSON, and XML within your shell scripts. These tools enhance your ability to extract specific information, filter data, transform structures, and automate data processing tasks, making your shell scripts more powerful and versatile for handling structured data.

7.3 Generating reports and visualizations: text-based reports and simple charts

Generating reports and visualizations from data is often necessary to communicate insights effectively. While shell scripting primarily focuses on text-based operations, you can still create basic reports and simple charts within your scripts. Let's explore these concepts:

Text-based reports:

- Shell scripting allows you to generate text-based reports by leveraging tools like echo, printf, and output redirection.
- You can format and display data in a structured manner using these commands, including headers, columns, and calculated values.
- By performing calculations, aggregations, and applying formatting rules, you can present data in a meaningful way within your reports.
- You can redirect the output of your script to a file for easy sharing or further processing.

Simple charts:

- While shell scripting doesn't provide built-in charting capabilities, you can create basic visualizations using ASCII characters or specialized tools.
- ASCII bar charts: You can represent data as vertical or horizontal bars using ASCII characters like | or #. Each character represents a value or a proportionate scale.
- Sparklines: Sparklines are small, inline charts that provide a visual representation of trends or patterns. You can use ASCII characters to plot simple line charts or bar charts.
- External tools: You can also integrate external tools like gnuplot or matplotlib into your shell scripts to generate more sophisticated charts.

These tools can create line charts, bar charts, scatter plots, and more, which can be saved as image files for inclusion in reports.

While text-based reports and simple charts may not offer the same level of visual sophistication as dedicated data visualization tools, they can still provide valuable insights and improve the readability of your shell script outputs. By creatively leveraging ASCII characters, formatting, and external tools, you can enhance the presentation of data and make your reports more informative and visually appealing.

Chapter 8: Scripting for Web Development

Web development is a dynamic and rapidly evolving field, and shell scripting can serve as a valuable tool in your web development workflow. In this chapter, we will explore how shell scripting can enhance your web development process, allowing you to automate tasks, manage web servers, interact with APIs, and streamline your development workflow.

We will begin by discussing the role of shell scripting in web development. You will learn how shell scripts can be used to automate repetitive tasks, such as file organization, project scaffolding, and build processes. We will explore techniques for creating scripts that generate project templates, manage dependencies, and automate the deployment of web applications.

Managing web servers is a crucial aspect of web development. We will cover techniques for configuring web servers, such as Apache or Nginx, using shell scripts. You will learn how to create scripts that automate server configuration, manage virtual hosts, and handle SSL/TLS certificate installation. Additionally, we will explore techniques for managing server logs, analyzing server performance, and automating backups.

Interacting with APIs is a common requirement in modern web development. We will discuss techniques for making HTTP requests, parsing JSON responses, and handling authentication using tools like curl and jq. You will learn how to create scripts that retrieve data from web APIs, automate data synchronization, and integrate external services into your web applications.

Version control is a critical component of collaborative web development. We will explore techniques for interacting with Git repositories using shell scripts. You will learn how to automate common version control tasks, such as branching, merging, and tagging, enabling you to streamline your development workflow and collaborate effectively with your team.

Shell scripting can also be used to automate testing and quality assurance in web development. We will cover techniques for automating the execution of unit tests, running code linters, and performing code analysis using tools like JUnit, ESLint, and SonarQube. By creating scripts that automate these processes, you can ensure code quality and detect potential issues early in the development cycle.

Throughout the chapter, we will emphasize best practices for secure and efficient web development scripting. You will learn about techniques for handling sensitive information, managing credentials securely, and protecting against common web vulnerabilities.

Additionally, we will explore ways to optimize your scripts for performance, scalability, and maintainability.

By the end of this chapter, you will have a solid understanding of how shell scripting can enhance your web development workflow. You will be equipped with the knowledge and tools to automate tasks, manage web servers, interact with APIs, and ensure code quality in your web applications. So, let's dive into Chapter 8: Scripting for Web Development and unlock the power of shell scripting in the dynamic world of web development. Get ready to supercharge your web development projects!

8.1 Web scraping and data extraction: using curl, wget, and regex

Web scraping and data extraction are common tasks in shell scripting, allowing you to retrieve information from websites. Tools like curl, wget, and regex patterns can be utilized to accomplish these tasks effectively. Let's explore these concepts in more detail:

curl:

- The curl command is a versatile tool for making HTTP requests and retrieving web content.

- Usage: curl [options] URL.
- You can use curl to download web pages, API responses, or other web resources.
- It supports various options like specifying request headers, handling cookies, and following redirects.
- By incorporating curl into your shell script, you can automate web content retrieval, save the response to a file, or extract specific data using further processing.

wget:

- wget is another command-line tool for retrieving files and web content.
- Usage: wget [options] URL.
- Similar to curl, wget supports downloading web pages, files, and resources.
- It includes options for recursive downloading, following links, and handling timeouts.
- By utilizing wget within your shell script, you can automate web content retrieval, download entire websites, or retrieve specific files from remote servers.

Regular expressions (regex):

- Regular expressions are powerful patterns used to match and extract specific content from text.

- Shell scripting languages like Bash provide support for regex patterns using built-in operators or tools like sed or awk.
- You can define regex patterns to match and extract data from the retrieved web content.
- By applying regex patterns in your shell script, you can extract specific information such as URLs, email addresses, or structured data from the web content.

When combined, curl, wget, and regex patterns enable you to automate web scraping and data extraction tasks within your shell scripts. You can retrieve web content, save it to files, and extract desired information using regex patterns. However, it is important to respect website terms of service and use web scraping responsibly and ethically.

8.2 Automating website testing: simulating user interactions with tools like Selenium

Automating website testing is a valuable task in ensuring the functionality and performance of web applications. While shell scripting is primarily focused on command-line operations, you can integrate tools like Selenium to simulate user interactions and automate website testing. Let's explore this concept in more detail:

Selenium:

- Selenium is a popular open-source framework for automating web browsers.
- It provides bindings for various programming languages, including Python, Java, and JavaScript.
- Selenium allows you to write scripts that simulate user interactions, such as clicking buttons, filling forms, and navigating through web pages.
- The WebDriver component of Selenium enables you to control web browsers programmatically and perform automated testing.
- By integrating Selenium with a supported programming language within your shell script, you can automate website testing tasks, interact with web elements, and validate expected behaviors.

Shell script integration:

- While shell scripting itself may not directly interact with web browsers, you can use shell scripting to orchestrate the execution of Selenium scripts.
- Shell scripts can handle tasks like invoking the Selenium test script, passing parameters, managing test data, and capturing test results.

- You can incorporate conditional statements, loops, and file operations within your shell script to enhance the automation and reporting capabilities of your website testing.

By integrating Selenium with shell scripting, you can automate website testing by simulating user interactions and validating the behavior of web applications. Shell scripting serves as the glue to coordinate and manage the execution of Selenium test scripts, allowing you to leverage the power of Selenium within your overall automation workflow.

8.3 Interacting with APIs: making HTTP requests and processing API responses

Interacting with APIs (Application Programming Interfaces) is a common task in shell scripting, allowing you to retrieve data, perform actions, and integrate with various services. You can make HTTP requests and process API responses using tools like curl and jq. Let's explore this concept in more detail:

Making HTTP requests:

- The curl command is a versatile tool for making HTTP requests and interacting with APIs.
- Usage: curl [options] URL.

- You can specify various HTTP methods like GET, POST, PUT, DELETE, etc., to perform different actions on the API.
- Additional options allow you to set headers, pass parameters, handle authentication, and handle response formats like JSON, XML, or plain text.
- By utilizing curl within your shell script, you can automate API requests, retrieve data, and capture the response for further processing.

Processing API responses:

- Once you receive the API response, you may need to process and extract specific information from it.
- The jq command-line tool is useful for parsing and manipulating JSON responses.
- Usage: jq '{filter}' API_response.json.
- You can use jq to extract values, filter data, transform structures, and perform calculations on JSON data.
- For non-JSON responses, you can use text processing tools like grep, sed, and awk to extract relevant information based on patterns or delimiters.

Authentication and authorization:

- Some APIs require authentication or authorization to access protected resources.

- curl supports various authentication methods like Basic Auth, OAuth, API keys, and tokens.
- You can include the necessary authentication headers or parameters in your curl command to authenticate with the API server.
- Additionally, you can handle authentication within your shell script by securely storing and retrieving credentials.

By combining tools like curl, jq, and text processing commands, you can interact with APIs, make HTTP requests, retrieve data, and process the API responses within your shell scripts. This allows you to automate tasks, integrate with external services, and extract specific information from API responses for further processing or analysis.

Chapter 9: Shell Scripting Best Practices

Shell scripting is a versatile and powerful tool, but writing efficient, secure, and maintainable scripts requires following best practices. In this chapter, we will explore a set of recommended practices and guidelines that will help you write high-quality shell scripts. By adhering to these best practices, you will create scripts that are reliable, efficient, and easy to understand and maintain.

Script Structure and Organization:

- Modularize your code into functions or separate scripts for better organization and reusability.
- Use meaningful and descriptive variable and function names to enhance code readability.
- Comment your code to provide explanations, document assumptions, and make it easier for others to understand and maintain the script.

Error Handling and Logging:

- Implement proper error handling techniques, such as checking command return codes and using conditional statements (if, else, fi) to handle errors gracefully.

- Log errors and informative messages to aid in troubleshooting and debugging. Utilize logging utilities or redirect output to log files.

Input Validation and Sanitization:

- Validate and sanitize user input to prevent unexpected behavior or security vulnerabilities. Use conditionals and input validation techniques to ensure the script operates with valid input.

Security Considerations:

- Avoid hardcoding sensitive information like passwords or API keys directly into scripts. Store such information securely, preferably in environment variables or separate configuration files.
- Validate and sanitize inputs to prevent command injection or other security vulnerabilities.
- Limit the execution permissions of your scripts to authorized users only.

Performance Optimization:

- Minimize unnecessary external command calls by leveraging built-in shell capabilities and native shell operations.

- Use appropriate command options and techniques to optimize script performance, especially when dealing with large datasets or resource-intensive operations.
- Consider utilizing parallel processing techniques or leveraging tools like xargs or parallel for improved performance.

Code Testing and Debugging:

- Write test cases and perform thorough testing of your scripts to ensure their functionality and reliability.
- Utilize debugging techniques and tools like set -x or bash -x script.sh to trace script execution and identify issues.
- Regularly review and refactor your code to eliminate redundancies and improve performance and readability.

Version Control and Collaboration:

- Use version control systems like Git to track changes, collaborate with others, and maintain a history of your script's development.
- Follow good version control practices, such as branching and merging strategies, commit conventions, and code review processes.

By adopting these shell scripting best practices, you can create scripts that are robust, efficient, and maintainable. Continuously strive to improve your scripting skills by staying updated with the latest shell scripting techniques and incorporating feedback from experienced shell scripters. Let Chapter 9: Shell Scripting Best Practices guide you towards writing shell scripts that excel in reliability, performance, security, and maintainability.

9.1 Writing clean and maintainable scripts: code formatting and commenting

Writing clean and maintainable shell scripts is essential for readability, collaboration, and long-term maintenance. Here are some practices for ensuring code formatting and adding meaningful comments:

Code Formatting:

- Use consistent indentation: Maintain a consistent indentation style, such as using tabs or spaces, to improve code readability.
- Line length: Keep lines within a reasonable length (usually 80-100 characters) to avoid horizontal scrolling and improve code clarity.
- Use meaningful variable names: Choose descriptive names for variables, functions, and constants to enhance code understanding.

- Organize code logically: Group related commands and functions together, and use whitespace to separate sections for better organization.

Adding Comments:

- Document script purpose: Include a brief comment at the beginning of your script explaining its purpose, author, and any relevant information.
- Function documentation: For complex functions or sections of code, add comments to describe their purpose, inputs, outputs, and any specific behavior.
- Comment important steps: Add comments before critical or complex steps to explain their purpose or provide context to future readers.
- Comment code reasoning: If a code snippet requires explanation or has a specific design choice, comment on the reasoning behind it to aid comprehension.
- Remove outdated comments: Regularly review and update comments to ensure they remain accurate and relevant.

Code Consistency:

- Stick to a style guide: If you're working in a team, follow a style guide or agreed-upon

conventions to ensure consistency across scripts.
- Regularly review and refactor: Take time to review your code periodically and refactor it for improved clarity and efficiency.
- Use version control: Utilize version control systems like Git to track changes, collaborate with others, and maintain a history of your script's evolution.

By following code formatting guidelines, adding meaningful comments, and promoting code consistency, you can write clean and maintainable shell scripts. These practices make your scripts easier to read, understand, and modify, facilitating collaboration among team members and reducing the likelihood of introducing errors during maintenance or updates.

9.2 Error handling and debugging: handling errors, logging, and troubleshooting

Error handling and debugging are crucial aspects of shell scripting to ensure robustness and ease troubleshooting. Consider the following practices:

Handling Errors:

- Use error checking and validation: Validate inputs, check command return codes, and handle potential errors or unexpected conditions appropriately.
- Use conditional statements: Employ if-else statements to check for errors and execute alternate code paths or display error messages.
- Exit codes: Set appropriate exit codes using the exit command to indicate the success or failure of the script or specific sections.
- Error messages: Provide informative error messages that describe the issue encountered and suggest potential solutions to assist in troubleshooting.

Logging and Debugging:

- Logging: Implement logging mechanisms to capture important events, error messages, and other relevant information during script execution. Redirect output to log files using the >> or 2>> redirection operators.
- Verbose mode: Consider adding a verbose mode to enable detailed logging or debug information when needed. It can be triggered by passing a command-line argument or setting an environment variable.
- Debugging tools: Utilize debugging tools like set -x or set -o xtrace to display each

command as it is executed, helping identify issues or unexpected behavior.
- Temporarily disable code: Comment out or remove specific sections of code to isolate problems and pinpoint their sources.

Error Recovery:

- Graceful exits: When encountering critical errors or exceptional conditions, ensure the script exits gracefully, cleaning up any resources or temporary files.
- Error notifications: Consider implementing a mechanism to notify relevant parties (such as administrators or users) about errors, either via email, system notifications, or logging to a central location.

Testing and Validation:

- Perform thorough testing: Test your script with different scenarios, including valid and invalid inputs, edge cases, and unexpected conditions, to ensure proper error handling.
- Use automated testing frameworks: Consider using testing frameworks like shUnit2 or Bats to automate the testing process and validate the expected behavior of your script.

By incorporating error handling techniques, logging mechanisms, and debugging practices, you can enhance the reliability and maintainability of your shell scripts. Robust error handling allows you to gracefully handle errors, facilitate troubleshooting, and ensure a smoother user experience.

9.3 Script optimization and performance considerations: improving execution speed and efficiency

Script optimization and considering performance aspects are essential for improving the execution speed and efficiency of shell scripts. Here are some practices to optimize your scripts:

Minimize system calls:

- Reduce the number of external commands and system calls by combining operations and utilizing built-in shell functionalities whenever possible.
- Utilize shell built-ins and features like parameter expansion, string manipulation, arithmetic operations, and pattern matching to minimize external command invocations.
- Use shell-specific features and constructs (e.g., process substitution, command substitution) to perform complex operations without spawning additional processes.

Efficient data processing:

- Optimize loops: Avoid unnecessary loops by using built-in commands like find, grep, or awk that can perform operations on multiple files or lines at once.
- Stream processing: Utilize the power of pipelines (|) to pass data between commands without creating intermediate files, reducing disk I/O and improving efficiency.
- Awk and Sed: Leverage the power of specialized tools like awk and sed for text processing tasks, as they are optimized for such operations.

Variable usage and scope:

- Minimize variable assignments: Reduce unnecessary variable assignments, especially within loops or repetitive sections, to optimize memory usage.
- Use local variables: Declare variables as local within functions or loops to limit their scope and avoid potential conflicts or unintended side effects.

Optimize file operations:

- Batch operations: Whenever possible, perform file operations (e.g., copying, moving, deleting)

in batches rather than individually, reducing system overhead.
- Efficient reading and writing: Use appropriate options and buffering mechanisms when reading or writing to files to minimize disk I/O operations.
- Consider using temporary files: If a script involves heavy file manipulation, consider using temporary files or in-memory storage to reduce disk I/O.

Profile and benchmark:

- Profile script execution: Use tools like time or dedicated profiling tools to identify performance bottlenecks and areas that require optimization.
- Benchmark different approaches: Test and compare alternative solutions or approaches to identify the most efficient ones for specific tasks.

Code review and refactoring:

- Regularly review your script code to identify areas for optimization or simplification.
- Refactor complex or repetitive sections into reusable functions to improve code clarity and execution efficiency.

By implementing these optimization practices, you can enhance the execution speed and efficiency of your shell scripts. However, it's important to balance optimization efforts with code readability and maintainability, ensuring that the script remains understandable and manageable in the long run.

Chapter 10: Real-world Examples and Case Studies

In this final chapter of the book, we will explore real-world examples and case studies that demonstrate the practical application of shell scripting in various domains. By examining these examples and case studies, you will gain valuable insights into how shell scripting can be used to solve complex problems, automate tasks, and streamline workflows in different scenarios.

System Administration Automation:

Explore a case study where shell scripting is utilized to automate system administration tasks, such as user management, software installation, and system monitoring. Learn how to create scripts that simplify administrative workflows and ensure system stability.

Log Analysis and Monitoring:

Dive into a real-world example of using shell scripting for log analysis and monitoring. Discover how to extract valuable information from system logs, detect patterns, generate reports, and set up automated alerts for critical events.

Data Processing and Transformation:

Examine a case study where shell scripting is employed to process and transform large datasets. Learn techniques for data extraction, cleansing, manipulation, and generating meaningful insights using shell scripting tools.

Web Scraping and Automation:

Explore how shell scripting can be leveraged for web scraping and automation tasks. Learn how to write scripts that extract data from websites, interact with web APIs, and automate repetitive web-based tasks.

Deployment and Continuous Integration:

Dive into a case study where shell scripting is used for deployment and continuous integration (CI). Discover how to automate the deployment of web applications, perform pre-deployment checks, and integrate shell scripts into CI/CD pipelines.

Network Monitoring and Security:

Explore a real-world example where shell scripting is employed for network monitoring and security. Learn how to create scripts that monitor network traffic, detect anomalies, and enhance network security through automation.

Task Automation and Productivity:

Examine various examples showcasing how shell scripting can improve productivity and automate everyday tasks. Discover scripts that streamline file organization, automate backups, facilitate data synchronization, and enhance personal workflow efficiency.

Through these real-world examples and case studies, you will gain practical knowledge and insights into the diverse applications of shell scripting. By understanding how shell scripting can be applied in different contexts, you will be inspired to explore new possibilities and tailor shell scripts to suit your specific needs.

As you delve into Chapter 10: Real-world Examples and Case Studies, take the opportunity to analyze, adapt, and expand upon the showcased examples to further enhance your shell scripting skills. By applying your creativity and problem-solving abilities, you can unlock the full potential of shell scripting in your own projects and scenarios. Let the real-world examples and case studies guide you on your journey towards becoming a proficient and resourceful shell scripter.

10.1 Case study 1: Automating backups and data synchronization with rsync

In this case study, we explore how to automate backups and data synchronization using the powerful utility rsync. Rsync is a versatile command-line tool that efficiently copies and synchronizes files between directories or across networks.

Problem:

- You need to back up important files and ensure they are synchronized across different locations or devices.
- Manually copying files is time-consuming and error-prone, especially when dealing with large or frequently changing data sets.
- You want to automate the backup process and ensure that only the modified or new files are transferred.

Solution:

Use rsync to automate backups and data synchronization with the following steps:

a. **Install rsync**: Ensure that rsync is installed on the system where the backup will be performed.

b. **Define source and destination**: Specify the source directory (the directory to be backed up) and the destination directory (where the backup will be stored).

c. **Set up the rsync command**: Construct an rsync command with appropriate options and parameters. For example:

- rsync -avz --delete source_directory/destination_directory
- The -a option preserves file permissions, timestamps, and other attributes during the transfer.
- The -v option enables verbose output to monitor the backup process.
- The -z option compresses data during transmission, reducing network bandwidth usage.
- The --delete option removes any files from the destination directory that no longer exist in the source directory, ensuring synchronization.

d. **Schedule automated backups**: Use cron or another scheduling tool to execute the rsync command at specified intervals. For example, running the backup script daily or weekly.

Benefits:

- **Automation**: The backup process is automated, eliminating the need for manual intervention and reducing the risk of human errors.

- **Incremental backups**: Rsync transfers only the modified or new files, minimizing network bandwidth usage and backup time.
- **Synchronization**: The --delete option ensures that the destination directory reflects the exact state of the source directory, keeping data synchronized.
- **Efficiency**: Rsync's efficient delta-transfer algorithm compares files and transfers only the portions that have changed, optimizing transfer speed.

Considerations:

- **Security**: Ensure appropriate access controls and permissions are in place to protect sensitive data during the backup process.
- **Network connectivity**: Reliable network connectivity is required for remote backups or data synchronization across networks.
- **Error handling**: Implement error handling mechanisms to capture and report any potential errors or failures during the backup process.
- **Logging**: Capture and store backup logs to facilitate monitoring and troubleshooting.

By leveraging rsync's capabilities, you can automate backups and data synchronization, ensuring that your important files are regularly backed up and efficiently synchronized across different locations or devices.

10.2 Case study 2: Creating a log analysis script with grep and awk

In this case study, we explore how to create a log analysis script using the powerful combination of grep and awk. Grep is a command-line utility for searching patterns in text, while awk is a versatile scripting language for text processing.

Problem:

You have a large log file containing valuable information, and you want to extract specific data and perform analysis on it.

Manually searching and parsing the log file is time-consuming and error-prone.

You want to automate the process of extracting relevant data from the log file and perform custom analysis on it.

Solution:

Use grep and awk to create a log analysis script with the following steps:

a. **Define log file and search pattern**: Specify the log file you want to analyze and identify the patterns you want to extract using grep. For example:

grep "pattern" log_file > extracted_data.txt

Replace "pattern" with the specific pattern you want to search for in the log file.

Redirect the output to a separate file (e.g., extracted_data.txt) for further processing.

b. **Use awk for data processing**: Construct an awk script to further process and analyze the extracted data. For example:

awk '{count[$1]++} END {for (word in count) print word, count[word]}' extracted_data.txt

The awk script uses an associative array (count) to count occurrences of specific data patterns (e.g., the first field $1 in the extracted data).

The END block is executed after processing all input lines, and it prints the unique data patterns and their respective counts.

c. **Customize analysis and output**: Modify the awk script to perform specific analysis or calculations based on your requirements. You can aggregate data, calculate statistics, or generate custom reports.

Benefits:

- **Automation**: The log analysis script automates the process of extracting and analyzing data from log files, saving time and effort.
- **Customization**: You can tailor the script to extract specific data patterns and perform custom analysis based on your needs.
- **Scalability**: The script can handle large log files efficiently, processing data line by line without overwhelming system resources.
- **Flexibility**: Grep and awk provide powerful text processing capabilities, allowing you to perform various operations on the extracted data.

Considerations:

- **Log file format**: Understand the log file format and the patterns you want to extract to ensure accurate data extraction and analysis.
- **Pattern selection**: Choose relevant and specific patterns to extract the desired data and avoid unnecessary information.
- **Error handling**: Implement error handling mechanisms to capture and handle any errors during the data extraction or analysis process.
- **Performance optimization**: Depending on the log file size, consider using appropriate options or techniques (e.g., line-by-line processing) to optimize the script's performance.

By leveraging the capabilities of grep and awk, you can create a powerful log analysis script to extract specific data patterns from log files and perform custom analysis. This automated approach saves time, allows for customization, and enables you to derive valuable insights from your log data.

10.3 Case study 3: Building a deployment pipeline with shell scripting and Git

In this case study, we explore how to build a deployment pipeline using shell scripting and Git, enabling continuous integration and automated deployments of software applications.

Problem:

You have a software application that undergoes frequent updates and requires a streamlined deployment process.

Manually deploying the application is time-consuming and error-prone, involving multiple steps and potential human errors.

You want to automate the deployment process and ensure consistent and efficient application deployments.

Solution:

Build a deployment pipeline using shell scripting and Git with the following steps:

a. **Version control with Git**: Set up a Git repository to manage your application's source code, including all the necessary files and configurations.

b. **Create deployment scripts**: Develop shell scripts that automate the deployment process, incorporating the necessary steps, such as building the application, copying files, configuring the environment, and restarting services.

c. **Continuous integration**: Integrate the deployment scripts into a continuous integration (CI) system, such as Jenkins or GitLab CI. Set up triggers to execute the deployment scripts automatically whenever there are new commits or specific branches are updated.

d. **Staging and production environments**: Configure separate staging and production environments to ensure proper testing and quality assurance before deploying to production.

e. **Define deployment stages**: Define different stages in the deployment pipeline, such as building, testing, staging, and production. Each stage executes specific deployment scripts and performs necessary checks or validations.

f. **Automate testing**: Integrate automated testing scripts into the pipeline to ensure the application's stability and functionality before deployment.

g. **Rollback mechanism**: Implement a rollback mechanism in case of deployment failures or issues. This can involve reverting to a previous working version or applying specific fixes.

h. **Logging and notifications**: Capture and store deployment logs to facilitate monitoring and troubleshooting. Set up notifications to alert the relevant stakeholders about deployment status and any failures.

Benefits:

- **Automation**: The deployment pipeline automates the entire deployment process, reducing manual effort and eliminating human errors.
- **Consistency**: The pipeline ensures consistent and reproducible deployments across different environments, reducing deployment-related issues.

- **Continuous integration**: By integrating with version control and CI systems, the pipeline enables continuous integration and faster feedback loops.
- **Scalability**: The pipeline can handle multiple application deployments simultaneously, accommodating a growing number of projects or teams.

Considerations:

- **Infrastructure as Code**: Consider utilizing infrastructure as code (IaC) tools like Ansible, Terraform, or Docker to automate infrastructure provisioning and ensure consistency between environments.
- **Security**: Implement secure practices, such as managing credentials, securing network communications, and applying necessary access controls to protect sensitive data.
- **Error handling**: Implement proper error handling mechanisms and logging to capture and handle deployment failures effectively.
- **Versioning**: Utilize version control tags or branches to track and manage different versions of your application.

By building a deployment pipeline with shell scripting and Git, you can automate the deployment process, enable continuous integration, and ensure consistent and efficient application deployments. This approach saves time, improves application quality, and enhances the overall development and deployment workflow.

Chapter 11: Advanced Shell Scripting Techniques

In this advanced chapter, we will explore a range of advanced shell scripting techniques that will elevate your scripting skills to the next level. These techniques will empower you to solve complex problems, handle challenging scenarios, and optimize your shell scripts for efficiency and versatility.

Advanced Flow Control:

Delve into advanced flow control constructs like case statements, nested loops, and advanced conditionals. Learn how to handle complex decision-making and create scripts that adapt to various scenarios.

Regular Expressions and Pattern Matching:

Master the art of regular expressions and pattern matching in shell scripting. Explore advanced techniques using tools like grep, sed, and awk to search, extract, and manipulate text based on specific patterns.

Advanced File Handling:

Discover advanced file handling techniques such as recursive file operations, file permissions manipulation, and file metadata extraction. Learn how to create scripts that efficiently traverse directories, manage file permissions, and gather file information.

Process Control and Job Management:

Explore techniques for process control and job management, including background processes, process manipulation, and signal handling. Learn how to create scripts that automate process management and handle complex job scenarios.

Script Optimization and Performance:

Learn strategies for optimizing shell script performance. Explore techniques such as caching, memoization, and algorithmic improvements to make your scripts run faster and more efficiently.

Advanced Text Processing:

Dive into advanced text processing techniques using tools like awk, sed, and tr. Discover how to perform advanced text transformations, data extraction, and manipulation tasks using powerful one-liners and scripting.

Interacting with Other Programming Languages:

Learn how to leverage shell scripting to interact with other programming languages. Explore techniques for calling external programs, utilizing shell scripts as glue code, and integrating with languages like Python, Perl, or Ruby.

Script Debugging and Troubleshooting:

Master advanced debugging and troubleshooting techniques for shell scripts. Learn how to use tools like set -x, strace, and valgrind to trace script execution, analyze system calls, and pinpoint script issues.

Creating Command-line Tools:

Explore techniques for creating command-line tools using shell scripting. Discover how to design user-friendly interfaces, handle command-line arguments, and package your scripts for distribution.

Script Security:

Enhance the security of your shell scripts by implementing secure coding practices. Explore techniques for preventing code injection, securing sensitive information, and protecting against common security vulnerabilities.

By diving into these advanced shell scripting techniques, you will expand your scripting repertoire and be equipped to tackle complex scripting challenges. Remember to apply these techniques judiciously and continuously seek opportunities to refine your scripting skills. Let Chapter 11: Advanced Shell Scripting Techniques be your guide as you push the boundaries of what can be accomplished with shell scripting. Embrace the power and flexibility of advanced shell scripting to create robust, efficient, and versatile solutions.

11.1 Advanced features of Bash scripting: arrays, functions, and process substitution

In this chapter, we explore advanced features of Bash scripting that enhance the power and flexibility of your shell scripts. We dive into three key topics: arrays, functions, and process substitution.

Arrays:

- **Understanding arrays**: Learn how to define and manipulate arrays in Bash scripts. Arrays allow you to store multiple values in a single variable, enabling efficient data organization and retrieval.
- **Array operations**: Explore various array operations such as adding or removing elements, accessing individual elements, iterating over array elements, and performing array-related calculations.

- **Associative arrays**: Discover associative arrays, which allow you to use arbitrary strings as array indices, enabling more complex data structures and key-value pairs.

Functions:

- **Creating functions**: Learn how to define and use functions in your scripts. Functions help modularize your code, improve reusability, and enhance script organization.
- **Function parameters**: Understand how to pass arguments to functions and how to access and process those arguments within the function.
- **Return values**: Explore techniques for returning values from functions, allowing you to capture and utilize the output of a function in other parts of your script.

Process Substitution:

- **Understanding process substitution**: Discover the concept of process substitution, which allows you to treat the output of a command or process as a file-like object within your script.
- **Command substitution vs. process substitution**: Learn the differences between command substitution and process substitution and when to use each technique.

- **Applications of process substitution**: Explore practical examples of how process substitution can be utilized, such as reading from multiple input sources, comparing command outputs, and passing command outputs as arguments.

By mastering arrays, functions, and process substitution in Bash scripting, you unlock advanced capabilities that empower you to write more sophisticated and efficient shell scripts. These features enable you to handle complex data structures, modularize your code, and integrate command outputs seamlessly. With these techniques at your disposal, you can take your Bash scripting skills to the next level and tackle more advanced scripting challenges with confidence.

11.2 Script modularity and code reuse: creating libraries and modular scripts

In this chapter, we delve into the importance of script modularity and code reuse in shell scripting. We explore techniques for creating libraries and modular scripts that enhance maintainability, reusability, and collaboration.

Understanding script modularity:

- **Modularity benefits**: Learn about the advantages of breaking down your scripts into modular components. Modularity improves code organization, readability, and ease of maintenance.
- **Separation of concerns**: Identify logical units within your script that can be encapsulated into separate modules, focusing on specific tasks or functionalities.
- **Modular design principles**: Explore design principles such as single responsibility, loose coupling, and high cohesion that contribute to well-structured modular scripts.

Creating libraries:

- **Library concept**: Understand the concept of libraries, which are collections of functions or utilities that can be shared across multiple scripts.
- **Library implementation**: Learn how to create reusable libraries by storing common functions or code snippets in separate script files.
- **Library usage**: Discover techniques for including and utilizing libraries within your scripts, enabling code reuse and avoiding duplication.

Building modular scripts:

- **Modular script structure**: Define a modular script structure that consists of reusable modules or functions, allowing for better organization and maintainability.
- **Inter-module communication**: Explore techniques for communication between modules, such as passing arguments, returning values, and utilizing shared variables or files.
- **Module testing and debugging**: Understand strategies for testing and debugging individual modules to ensure their correctness and troubleshoot any issues.

Collaboration and code sharing:

- **Version control**: Integrate your modular scripts and libraries with version control systems like Git to facilitate collaboration, track changes, and manage different versions.
- **Documentation**: Emphasize the importance of documenting your libraries and modular scripts to provide clear instructions and usage examples for other developers.
- **Sharing and distribution**: Explore options for sharing your libraries and modular scripts with the wider community, such as publishing them on code repositories or package managers.

By adopting a modular approach and creating libraries in your shell scripting, you can improve code organization, promote code reuse, and facilitate collaboration among developers. Modular scripts and libraries enhance the maintainability and scalability of your scripts, allowing for more efficient development and reducing duplication of effort. With these techniques, you can harness the power of modularity to build robust and reusable shell scripts.

11.3 Scripting for security and defensive programming: input validation and secure coding practices

In this chapter, we focus on the crucial aspects of security and defensive programming in shell scripting. We explore techniques for input validation and secure coding practices to mitigate common security vulnerabilities and ensure the robustness of your scripts.

Importance of input validation:

- **Understanding input validation**: Recognize the significance of validating user input and external data to prevent security breaches and mitigate the risk of malicious attacks.
- **Input validation vulnerabilities**: Learn about common vulnerabilities such as command

injection, SQL injection, and code injection that can result from inadequate input validation.

Techniques for input validation:

- **Sanitizing input**: Implement techniques to sanitize and validate user input, including input from command-line arguments, environment variables, and user prompts.
- **Regular expressions**: Utilize regular expressions to define patterns and validate input against predefined criteria.
- **Whitelisting and blacklisting**: Employ whitelisting and blacklisting approaches to define allowed and disallowed characters or patterns for input validation.

Secure coding practices:

- **Principle of least privilege**: Follow the principle of least privilege by ensuring that your scripts only have the necessary permissions and privileges to execute their intended tasks.
- **Secure variable handling**: Implement secure practices for handling sensitive data, such as passwords and API keys, by avoiding storing them in plain text and using secure methods for accessing and manipulating them.
- **Secure file operations**: Employ secure file handling techniques, such as checking file

permissions, validating file paths, and preventing directory traversal attacks.
- **Error handling and logging**: Implement robust error handling mechanisms to handle unexpected situations gracefully, avoiding the exposure of sensitive information, and logging errors securely.
- **Input/output validation**: Validate input and output data from external sources, such as network connections or system commands, to prevent security breaches and ensure the integrity of your script's execution.

Continuous security improvements:

- **Regular security audits**: Conduct regular security audits of your scripts, reviewing and updating input validation techniques and secure coding practices.
- **Staying updated:** Keep yourself informed about the latest security vulnerabilities, patches, and best practices relevant to shell scripting.
- **Collaboration and knowledge sharing**: Engage with the wider developer community, participate in security forums, and share knowledge about secure coding practices to benefit from collective expertise.

By incorporating input validation techniques and following secure coding practices, you can significantly enhance the security and resilience of your shell scripts. Implementing these measures helps protect your scripts and systems from potential security threats, safeguard sensitive data, and build trust in the reliability of your applications. Prioritizing security and defensive programming ensures that your scripts are robust, secure, and able to withstand potential attacks.

Chapter 12: Beyond Shell Scripting

In this final chapter of the book, we will explore various tools and technologies that go beyond traditional shell scripting and expand your horizons as a developer. These tools and technologies will complement your shell scripting skills and enable you to tackle complex tasks and solve divorce problems in innovative ways.

Configuration Management Tools:

Discover powerful configuration management tools like Ansible, Chef, and Puppet. Learn how these tools can automate infrastructure provisioning, configuration management, and application deployment, going beyond the capabilities of shell scripting alone.

Containerization and Orchestration:

Dive into the world of containerization and orchestration with tools like Docker and Kubernetes. Explore how these technologies provide scalable, portable, and isolated environments for deploying and managing applications, revolutionizing the way software is developed and deployed.

Scripting in Other Languages:

Explore scripting in other languages, such as Python, Ruby, or Perl, which offer extensive libraries, frameworks, and language features for various domains. Discover how to leverage the strengths of these languages to complement your shell scripting skills and solve complex tasks efficiently.

Task Automation Frameworks:

Delve into task automation frameworks like Make, Rake, or Grunt. Learn how these frameworks provide powerful task management capabilities, allowing you to automate build processes, task dependencies, and complex workflows efficiently.

Cloud Infrastructure and DevOps Tools:

Explore cloud infrastructure and DevOps tools like AWS CLI, Terraform, and Jenkins. Discover how these tools can automate cloud resource management, infrastructure provisioning, and continuous integration and delivery, enabling you to build scalable and robust systems.

Data Processing and Analysis Tools:

Dive into data processing and analysis tools like Apache Spark, Hadoop, or Pandas. Learn how these tools enable efficient processing and analysis of large datasets, making it easier to derive meaningful insights and make data-driven decisions.

Web Frameworks and APIs:

Explore web frameworks and APIs like Flask, Express, or Django. Discover how these frameworks simplify web development, allowing you to build robust, scalable, and feature-rich web applications with ease.

Database Management and Querying:

Delve into database management and querying tools like SQL, NoSQL databases, or ORM frameworks. Learn how to interact with databases, design efficient queries, and leverage the power of databases in your applications.

Machine Learning and AI:

Discover the field of machine learning and AI and explore libraries like TensorFlow, PyTorch, or scikit-learn. Learn how to leverage machine learning algorithms and models to solve complex problems and make predictions based on data.

Continuous Integration and Deployment:

Explore continuous integration and deployment tools like Jenkins, GitLab CI/CD, or Travis CI. Learn how to automate the build, testing, and deployment processes of your applications, ensuring efficient and reliable software delivery.

By exploring these tools and technologies beyond shell scripting, you will broaden your skill set and be prepared to tackle a wide range of development tasks. Embrace the versatility and power of these tools to build robust, scalable, and efficient solutions that go beyond the limits of traditional shell scripting. Let Chapter 12: Beyond Shell Scripting be your guide as you venture into the exciting realm of advanced development tools and technologies.

12.1 Integration with other scripting languages and tools: using Python, Perl, or Ruby

In this final chapter, we explore the possibilities of integrating shell scripting with other popular scripting languages such as Python, Perl, or Ruby. By combining the strengths of different scripting languages, you can leverage a wider range of tools and functionalities to enhance your scripting capabilities.

Benefits of integration:

Expanding functionality: Understand the advantages of integrating shell scripting with other languages, enabling you to access their extensive libraries and features.

Task specialization: Identify tasks that can be better accomplished using a specific scripting language, such as complex data processing, web scraping, or text manipulation.

Integration techniques:

- **Invoking external scripts**: Learn how to call scripts written in other languages from within your shell script, passing data between the two languages and utilizing their respective capabilities.
- **Inter-process communication**: Explore techniques for establishing communication channels between shell scripts and scripts in other languages, allowing them to exchange data and work collaboratively.
- **Utilizing language-specific libraries**: Take advantage of language-specific libraries or modules in Python, Perl, or Ruby by incorporating them into your shell scripts, unlocking advanced functionality and simplifying complex tasks.

Practical examples:

- **Python integration**: Discover how to leverage the power of Python within your shell scripts, using its rich ecosystem of libraries for tasks such as data analysis, web scraping, or interacting with APIs.
- **Perl integration**: Explore how Perl can complement shell scripting with its strong text-processing capabilities, regular expression support, and extensive collection of modules for various domains.
- **Ruby integration**: Learn how to integrate Ruby into your shell scripts, tapping into its elegant syntax, object-oriented features, and libraries for tasks like web development, system administration, or automation.

Best practices and considerations:

- **Compatibility and dependencies**: Consider compatibility issues and ensure that the required scripting language and its dependencies are available on the target system.
- **Error handling and debugging**: Address potential challenges related to error handling, debugging, and troubleshooting when integrating multiple scripting languages.
- **Documentation and maintainability**: Emphasize the importance of documenting integration points, dependencies, and any

language-specific code to ensure maintainability and facilitate collaboration.

By exploring the integration of shell scripting with other scripting languages like Python, Perl, or Ruby, you open up new possibilities for expanding the functionality and versatility of your scripts. Leveraging the strengths of different languages allows you to tackle complex tasks more efficiently and tap into the extensive libraries and tools available in each language's ecosystem. By combining the powers of shell scripting and other scripting languages, you can create powerful, flexible, and robust solutions that meet a wider range of requirements.

12.2 Creating shell script-based applications: packaging scripts as executables

In this chapter, we explore the process of transforming your shell scripts into standalone, executable applications. By packaging your scripts as executables, you can distribute them more conveniently, enhance their portability, and provide a user-friendly experience for running your scripts.

Benefits of packaging as executables:

- **Simplified execution**: Understand how packaging your scripts as executables eliminates the need for users to have a shell interpreter installed and allows them to run your scripts directly.
- **Enhanced portability**: Learn how executable packages can be deployed across different operating systems and environments without dependencies on specific shell interpreters or libraries.
- **User-friendly experience**: Provide users with a seamless, executable format that simplifies the execution of your scripts and shields them from underlying technical details.

Packaging techniques:

- **Shell script wrappers**: Explore the concept of creating a wrapper script that embeds your original shell script and sets up the necessary environment to execute it.
- **Compiler tools**: Discover tools such as shc, shcomp, or batsh that can compile your shell scripts into binary executables, reducing the dependency on shell interpreters.
- **Packaging frameworks**: Explore existing frameworks like Makeself or Bash-Scripts-Toolbox that facilitate the creation of self-extracting archives or installation packages for your scripts.

Distribution considerations:

- **Target platforms**: Determine the target platforms for your executable packages, considering the operating systems and architectures you wish to support.
- **Dependencies**: Ensure that any external dependencies required by your scripts are bundled or made available alongside the executable, minimizing the need for manual installations.
- **Security considerations**: Implement security measures, such as code signing or digital signatures, to verify the authenticity and integrity of your executable packages.

User interaction and customization:

- **Command-line interfaces**: Design user-friendly command-line interfaces (CLIs) that allow users to interact with your scripts easily, providing clear instructions, help messages, and options.
- **Configuration files**: Explore techniques for incorporating configuration files that allow users to customize the behavior of your executable scripts without modifying the script itself.

Updating and maintenance:

- **Versioning**: Implement versioning mechanisms to track changes and updates to your executable scripts, enabling users to identify and download newer versions.
- **Error handling and logging**: Ensure robust error handling and logging mechanisms within your executable scripts to facilitate debugging and troubleshooting.

By packaging your shell scripts as executables, you can provide users with a convenient and portable way to run your scripts without the need for shell interpreters. Executable packages simplify the distribution process, enhance the user experience, and increase the portability of your scripts across different platforms. Whether it's through shell script wrappers, compiler tools, or packaging frameworks, transforming your scripts into executables opens up new possibilities for deploying and sharing your shell-based applications.

12.3 Exploring advanced automation frameworks: Ansible, Chef, and Puppet

In this chapter, we delve into advanced automation frameworks that go beyond shell scripting: Ansible, Chef, and Puppet. These frameworks provide powerful tools for managing and automating complex infrastructure configurations, deployments, and system administration tasks.

Introduction to automation frameworks:

- **Understanding the need for automation**: Explore the reasons why automation frameworks have gained popularity in managing large-scale infrastructures and repetitive tasks.
- **Key features and benefits**: Learn about the key features and benefits offered by automation frameworks, including declarative configuration management, idempotent operations, and infrastructure as code.

Ansible:

- **Overview and architecture**: Get an overview of Ansible and its architecture, including the use of YAML-based playbooks and the agentless nature of Ansible.
- **Playbook development**: Dive into writing Ansible playbooks to define and automate various tasks, including configuration management, application deployments, and system orchestration.
- **Inventory management**: Explore techniques for managing inventory, organizing hosts into groups, and handling variables for targeted automation.

- **Ansible roles**: Discover the concept of roles in Ansible, enabling modular and reusable automation configurations.

Chef:

- **Introduction to Chef**: Understand the principles and components of Chef, including the use of a domain-specific language (DSL) for defining infrastructure as code.
- **Cookbook development**: Learn how to write Chef cookbooks to define recipes, resources, and dependencies for configuring and managing systems.
- **Node management**: Explore Chef's node management capabilities, including bootstrapping new nodes, managing node attributes, and applying configurations to specific nodes or groups.
- **Chef server and Chef workstation**: Gain insights into the role of the Chef server and workstation in managing infrastructure and facilitating collaboration.

Puppet:

- **Puppet overview**: Get acquainted with Puppet and its approach to configuration management using a declarative language.
- **Puppet manifests**: Explore writing Puppet manifests to define resource configurations,

dependencies, and the desired state of systems.
- **Puppet modules**: Understand the concept of Puppet modules for organizing and sharing reusable configurations, extending Puppet's functionality, and promoting code reusability.
- **Puppet server and agent**: Learn about the Puppet server-agent architecture and the communication process between them for enforcing configurations.

Choosing the right automation framework:

- **Considerations and use cases**: Evaluate factors such as scalability, complexity, existing infrastructure, and community support to determine which automation framework is suitable for your specific use cases.
- **Integration with shell scripting**: Discover how shell scripting can complement and extend the capabilities of automation frameworks, allowing you to leverage existing scripts and tools.

By exploring advanced automation frameworks like Ansible, Chef, and Puppet, you can take your automation efforts to the next level. These frameworks offer robust tools and methodologies for managing infrastructure configurations, deployments, and system administration tasks. Understanding the architecture, developing playbooks or cookbooks, and leveraging the strengths of each framework allows you to automate complex tasks effectively and maintain consistent configurations across your infrastructure.

"Shell Scripting in Action: Real-world Examples and Case Studies" is a comprehensive guide that equips readers with the skills and knowledge to harness the power of shell scripting in practical contexts. Authored by Owen Ford, this book takes readers on a journey through the world of shell scripting, providing hands-on examples and case studies that showcase the real-world applications of this versatile scripting language.

The book begins with an introduction to the fundamentals of shell scripting, including an overview of different shell environments and guidance on setting up the shell environment. From there, readers delve into essential topics such as variables, control flow, file and directory operations, and text processing. Through clear explanations and step-by-step instructions, readers gain proficiency in automating system tasks, managing processes and services, and monitoring system resources.

The exploration of shell scripting extends to networking, as readers learn to automate network-related tasks, retrieve information from remote servers, and troubleshoot network issues using powerful scripting techniques. The book further delves into the realm of data analysis, demonstrating how shell scripts can be employed to process and analyze data files, work with different data formats, and generate reports and visualizations.

With an eye toward web development, the book reveals how shell scripting can be used for web scraping, website testing, and interacting with APIs, offering readers the tools to automate tasks and streamline their web-related workflows. Throughout the chapters, readers are guided by best practices for writing clean and maintainable scripts, as well as techniques for error handling, debugging, and script optimization.

The book concludes with a focus on advanced shell scripting techniques, empowering readers to leverage features such as arrays, functions, and process substitution. It also explores script modularity, code reuse, and security considerations to further enhance their scripting skills. Additionally, readers discover avenues for integration with other scripting languages and tools, and explore the possibilities of creating shell script-based applications and leveraging automation frameworks.

By the end of "Shell Scripting in Action: Real-world Examples and Case Studies," readers are equipped with a robust skill set that allows them to apply shell scripting to a wide range of real-world scenarios. With its practical approach, this book serves as a valuable resource for system administrators, developers, and anyone seeking to unlock the full potential of shell scripting in their day-to-day work.

Unleash the power of shell scripting and revolutionize your approach to automation and efficiency with **"Shell Scripting in Action: Real-world Examples and Case Studies."**

www.ingramcontent.com/pod-product-compliance
Lightning Source LLC
Chambersburg PA
CBHW071511220526
45472CB00003B/987